This Heavenly Wine

This Heavenly Wine

Poetry from the Divan-e Jami

by

Nooreddin Abdurrahman

Ibn-e Ahmad-e Jami

Renditions by Vraje Abramian

Hohm Press

Prescott, Arizona

Cover design: Massoud Mansori
Layout and design: Tori Bushert

Library of Congress Cataloging-in-Publication Data

Jami, 1414-1492.
    [Poems. English. Selections]
    This heavenly wine : renditions from Divan-e Jami / by Nooreddin
Abdurrahman Ibn-e Ahmad-e Jami ; renditions by Vraje Abramian.
        p. cm.
    Translations from Persian.
    Includes bibliographical references.
    ISBN 1-890772-56-9 (pbk. : alk. paper)
    I. Abramian, Vraje. II. Title.
    PK6490.A2 2006
    891'.5512—dc22
                        2006008701

HOHM PRESS
P.O. Box 2501
Prescott, AZ 86302
800-381-2700
http://www.hohmpress.com

This book was printed in the U.S.A. on acid-free paper using soy ink.

10 09 08 07 06   5 4 3 2 1

Poem appearing on the cover is from *Divan-e Jami*, Book I, p. 691, no. 774.

To Huzur
the Wineseller of Beas
the Perfect Friend

ଓଃ

away from You
I am fed up with my existence Friend
I can bear being away from all and everyone
separation from You is beyond me, Friend

whenever we come together
I want to read You my book of sorrows
but long before I get near there
I lose my speech, Friend

You ask me how my heart feels
how could I know anything about my heart
it has for so long been sitting at your feet,
    Friend

do not send me away
for all I wish to do with my life
is to offer that too at Your feet, Friend

—Jami

My sincere thanks to Regina Sara Ryan for all she has done; to my wife, Elizabeth, for her immense patience and support; and to Mr. Massoud Mansori, for who he is, and for his masterful artwork, which adorns the cover of this book as well as the cover of *Nobody, Son of Nobody*, Hohm Press, 2001.

CONTENTS

happy are two wayfarers
who in this foreign land of trials
chance upon each other and relish a few moments
speaking of their Longing for their Home

—Jami

ᦂ

drop all coverings and bring along your lovesick heart
then you may walk in Love's company

be erased from your own being and surrender
shadowlessly walk in Love's company

better to willingly choose to be dust in this Love
for eventually there'll be no choice, only dust

—Jami

INTRODUCTION

Mystics and Poetry

The purpose of birth is learning.
The purpose of learning is to grasp the divine.[1]

The greatest impediment to the human
spirit results from the fact that
the conception of God is fixed in a
particular form, due to childish habit
and imagination.[2]

The Infinite transcends every particular
content of faith.[3]

—Kabbalah

It is said that true mystics are individuals who are united with that Presence from whom all creation emanates, has its life in, and to whom it returns. The timeless, placeless state of

---

[1]Matt, Daniel C. *The Essential Kabbalah: The Heart of Jewish Mysticism*. Edison, New Jersey: Castle Books, 1997, 21.
[2]Ibid., 33.
[3]Ibid., 35.

being that mystics refer to does not easily fit into our place/time dominated understanding of existence. They tell us that whatever our questions, we can satisfy them through personal experience if we follow a way of life that they practice: "...offer your soul at the Beloved's feet / in order for your lot to be Love at the end / rather than separation and despair," writes Sheikh Fakhreddin Eraqi.[4]

These mystics tell us that, while in human form, we have the potential to awaken and begin a journey in the direction of completion and fulfillment by personally experiencing that Infinite Presence our essence is made of.

One medium used by mystics to express verbally and to speak to the masses particularly in the Middle East and the Indian sub-continent, has been poetry. Poetry is the language of intimacy, and intimacy with the Divine generates divine poetry. Those who dare, and are granted divine intimacy, do not limit themselves to the idea of a relationship between sovereign and subject, or any other self-imposed taboos. This relationship, rather than being a calculated service in the hope of worldly and/or heavenly gains, is one in which love, left in trust in the heart of the individual, seeks to return and be fulfilled in the source of love, the Beloved. Poetry flowing through the hearts of mystics, whether a lamentation bemoaning separation, a drunken boasting of the Beloved's infinite splendor or a whisper before extinction in union, is said to originate with the Beloved and is in return offered at the feet of the Beloved.

[4]Mohtasham, Dr. Nasrin (Khazai). *Works of Fakhreddin Eraqi*. In Farsi. Tehran, Iran: Zavvar Publications, 1966, 26-28, lines 194-208, selected. Translated from the Farsi by Vraje Abramian.

Statements made by mystics from different places and times speak of the pain of longing for nearness and the agony/bliss when nearness is granted. They speak of the pain-ridden ecstasy of a drop stretching to contain the ocean and "dying" in the process; for that is the only way the drop may leave its limitations behind and become infinity. In like-minded hearts these poems trigger ecstasy, they also cause perfumed spring showers and rejuvenate parched souls crossing the vast, unmapped deserts of seeking.

Seeking the One who cannot be "named," the One whose pull one has died many deaths trying to resist, the One in separation from whom one agonizes like a fish on hot sand and in whose nearness one sinks like a shipwreck being swallowed deep into the bottomless.

These poems can also make some wonder about the "sanity" of the author, like Baba Taher-e Oryan, who wrote: "...everyone's pain leads / to some cure someday / except this pain in my heart / which seeks more pain / for its cure"[5]; and St. John of the Cross who wrote, "I begged love to kill me / since he wounded me so deeply / and I leaped into the fire / knowing I would burn completely..."[6]

An onlooker, who has lived on the shore of an ocean he has never swam in, will certainly find strange and incoherent the

---

[5]Masoomi, Reeza, *Jami az Oqianoose Beekarane Erfan* (*Selections of Mystic Poetry, a Cup from the Infinite Ocean of Gnosi*), 6th edition, Tehran, Iran: Nashre-Eshare Publications, 1991, original Farsi. English translation by Vraje Abramian.
[6]de Nicholas, Antonio T. *Saint John of the Cross, Alchemist of the Soul: His Life His Poetry (Bilingual) His Prose*. Foreword by Seyyed Hossein Nasr. New York: Paragon House, 1989. "Not for all the beauty," page 144.

manners of one who, having crossed the vastest, hottest stretches of the loneliest desert, tears off all his clothes and, embraced all over by water, screams in delirious joy. So be it.

The Sufis

In Iran those who have developed this intimacy with the Beloved are often referred to as Sufis[7] and poetry is their favorite medium of expression. In over five hundred years, from Sheikh Abu-Saeed Abil-Kheir (967-1049), a Sufi poet who is said to have influenced later giants such as Sanai, Attar and Rumi, to Nureddin Abdorrahman Ibn-e Ahmad Jami (1414-1492), known by some as Khatam-ol-Shoara (the final poet),[8] Sufis created an immense wealth of delicately refined, spiritual expression in verse so powerful as to impact every culture it has come in contact with.

As Dr. Seyyed Hossein Nasr puts it, Persian language was "...strengthened by the use of Quranic terminology and Arabic vocabulary. This immensely delicate and versatile language soon developed a literature of vast dimensions...Especially in

---

[7]For a complete description of Sufis and Sufism, please see Dr. Javad Nurbaksh's Foreword to *Classical Persian Sufism: From Its Origins to Rumi*, xv-xxxix. For a thorough, meticulously-researched history and background on Persian Sufism, see "The Rise and Development of Persian Sufism," by Dr. S. H. Nasr, in *Classical Persian Sufism: From Its Origins to Rumi*, edited by Leonard Lewisohn, Article 1, 1993, pp. 1-18.
[8]For he was "the final one in the golden era of classic...Sufi poetry which produced the likes of Saadi, Nizami, Hafiz, Khayyam, Rumi and Attar to name but a few" (Afsahzad, 99).

relation to Sufism, Persian literature gave birth to incomparable Sufi poetry, which carried the Persian language to the farthest confines of India and western China and the Ottoman Empire as far west as Albania. For many centuries Persian was the lingua franca of most of Asia…a language whose crown of glory is Sufi poetry." (SHN, 1975)

People of diverse tongues and backgrounds have made Persian poetry their own. The Whirling Dervishes of Anatolia have turned to Molana Jalal-eddin's moanings. In Caucasus, Armenian and Georgian bards, like the Georgian-Armenian minstrel Sayat Nova, buried in the Armenian cemetery in Tbilisi, have made Nizami, Hafez and Khayyam theirs, singing their love stories. Azeries, Tajiks and Uzbegs, from Samarqhand and Bokhara to Kashqar in western China, through their bards and Khojas (from Persian, *Khaja* = master), have instructed and entertained, using works from Nizami, Khaje Abdollah Ansari, Khaqani, Rudaki and others.

In regions known today as Pakistan, Afghanistan, Sindh and Punjab, Qawwals[9] (Muslim devotional singers), to whom Jami is a favorite, have for centuries used Sufi poetry to bring crowds to ecstasy. All of these nations have been recipients of, and contributors to, a poetic tradition in Persian coming from a culture "so deeply rooted in poetic expression that one might call it a bardic civilization." (Wilson and Pourjavadi, 1987)

---

[9]Of the many Sufi-inspired devotional singers (Qawwals), Nosrat Fateh Ali Khan and Sabri Brothers, and Abida Parveen, "The Daughter of the Dargah," are relatively well known in the West.

In the West, though some of the most famous Sufi poets, such as Rumi, Hafez and Khayyam, are well known and appreciated, many have barely been introduced. One such giant is Nureddin Abdorrahman Ibn-e Ahmad Jami whose works have inspired poets, mystics, and Qawwals as well as laymen and women.

Jami: A Short Biography

Nureddin Abdorrahman Ibn-e Ahmad Jami was born in Khargerd, Jam,[10] in the eastern province of Khorasan,[11] Iran, on November 7, 1414 AD (23 Shabaan 817 AH). His father Nizamoddin Ahmad Dashti was from Dasht-e Esfahan; he was an educated man and well known in Khorasan, and many Sufis visited his place.

Like many other mystics in the region, Jami's life and his statements are often recounted.[12] One anecdote that might be rather illuminating is that one day a disciple asked for a piece of advice to carry on the path. Jami, it is said, laid his hand on his breast and said, "It's here...you will find everything here."

When Jami was five, Parsa Abdorrahman, the Naqshbandi

---

[10]*Jam* rhymes with "jam" (as in strawberry jam). His pen name Jami, pronounced Jaami (rhymes with Tommy) derives from his place of birth. *Jaam* also means wine goblet, the basis of many of the puns Jami uses in his poetry.

[11]Today, the northeastern Iranian province of Khorasan borders Afghanistan. In the sixteenth century it denoted a much vaster region which embraced western Afghanistan, as well as a major part of Trans-Oxanian Central Asia, present day Turkmenistan, Tajikistan and Uzbbekistan.

master, was passing through Jam on his way to Hejaz. Jami was taken to the master by his father to receive blessings. Sixty years later Jami would write:

...my heart still feels the joy I experienced from that happy

meeting. I firmly believe that that bond of friend-
ship...and love

which subsequently bound the great body of pious spir-
its to this

humble creature, is wholly due to the fortunate influ-
ence of his glance...

(F. Hadland Davis, 1980)[13]

Jami received his early education from his father and at age thirteen went to Herat (in present day Afghanistan), which was one of the main cultural and educational centers of the Muslim world, for further studies. There he studied with Joneid Osouli and soon became known for his exceptional talents in logic, languages and sciences. At around age twenty, he moved to Samarqhand (present day Tajikistan) to study with Qhazizade Rumi who was a scientist at Ologh Beg Observatory there.

---

[12]For a rather comprehensive analysis of Jami's character and personali-
ty, see David Pendelbury's Afterword in *Yusuf and Zulaikha*, an alle-
gorical romance by Hakim Nureddin Abdurrahman Jami, edited,
abridged and translated by David Pendlebury, The Octagon Press,
London, 1980. Farsi readers may consult Afsahzad's volume on Jami's
biography, pp. 22-305 (see Bibliography).
[13]Davis, F. Hadland. *The Persian Mystics*. London, John Murray, 1908.
Wisdom of the East Series, 14.

Qhazizade was so impressed by Jami's performance that in a gathering he declared:

> ...for as long as this city has stood, no one as sharp and as learned as this youth from Jam has crossed the Amooy (Oxus) river to Samarqhand...
>
> (Heravi, 1998)[14]

By his late thirties, Jami was respected in the vast Muslim lands of the mid-fifteenth century as one of the most cultured and learned personalities of his time. It is said that in Samarqhand, while nursing his broken heart after a romantic affair, Jami was visited in a dream by a luminous figure who advised him thus:

> ...brother, go find a beloved who can not abandon you...
>
> (Heravi, 1998)[15]

Taking these words to heart, Jami returned to Herat and began frequenting Sufi places of gathering, or Khaneqhahs. At age forty he was initiated into the brotherhood by the Naqshbandi master of Khorasan, Saadeddin Kashqari, the luminous visitor in Jami's dream!

The secular circles in Samarqhand and Herat were apparently so shocked that one of their number had joined the mystics

---

[14]Heravi, Najib Mayel. *Sheikh Abdorrahman Jami*. In Farsi. Tehran, Iran: Tarh-e No Publications, 1998, 35.
[15]Ibid., page 36.

that a well-known scholar, Shahabeddin Mohammad Jajermi declared:

...in these five hundred years,
one truly learned among the educated of Khorasan
appeared and was snatched by Master Kashqari...
(Heravi, 1998)[16]

Another declared:

...I would never have believed that there was
anything higher than learning and proven scholarship
had I not seen Jami join
the ranks of Sufis...
(Heravi, 1998)[17]

Proving equally dedicated at spiritual practice, at age forty-three Jami received the permission from his master, Kashqari to guide seekers:

"...who had received it from Nizamoddin Khamoosh,
who had received it from Alaoddin Attar, who had
received it from the founder of the order,
Bahaoddin Naqhsband directly..."
(Afsahzad, 1999)[18]

---

[16]Ibid., page 38.
[17]Ibid., page 38.
[18]Afsahzad, Ala Khan. *A Critical Study of Jami's Biography and Writings*. Under the supervision of the Written Heritage Publication Office, Center for Iranian Studies, Tehran, 1999, pp. 313-331.

Though he was sought after by many rulers in the Muslim lands of his time, Jami chose a quiet life in Herat, where he lived until his death on November 9, 1492 (18 Maharam, 898 AH).

Jami authored forty-six major literary works, including *Leily-o-Majnoon*, *Salaman-o-Absal* and *Yoosef-o-Zoleikha*, which are love stories recast in Jami's style; *Kheradname-e Eskandari* (*The Alexandrine Book of Wisdom*) a book of counsel and advice to rulers that utilizes the Macedonian's historic popularity to champion the idyllic ruler; and *Nafahat-ol-Uons*, a book on the lives of 616 Sufis, including 34 Sufi women.

Divan-e Jami was completed in 1489, three years before the author's death. The original compilation is in three parts: *Faatahat-ol Shabub; Vasetat-ol Aqhd;* and *Kahatmat-ol Hayat*: reflections on youth, maturity and old age. The collection presented here comes from Ala Khan Afsahzad's three-volume set.[19]

A Word on "Translation" and "Rendition"

Farsi (Persian) is not a language that lends itself to translation easily. Persian poetry by Sufi mystics often combines multi-layered content with awe-inspiringly polished form. It

---

[19]Ibid. Ala Khan Afsahzad edited Jami's original works held in the following repositories: the Iranian National Library, Tehran, The Islamic Republic of Iran; the Department of Oriental Studies, Academy of Sciences of the University of St. Petersburg; Oriental Manuscripts Deposit, Academy of Sciences, the Republic of Uzbekistan; Oriental Manuscript Deposit Academy of Sciences, the Republic of Tajikstan; Manuscript Trust, Academy of Sciences, the Republic of Azerbaijan and Saltikef Shidrin Manuscript Trust, Public Library of St. Petersburg.

also draws on, and is informed by, a collective consciousness at least one thousand years old, and one so saturated by Sufi cosmology, and its many-layered manifestations, that it would not be an exaggeration to say that Sufism provides the backbone to the Iranian culture. Adepts in using metaphors, imagery and all shades of meaning in spiritual and secular contexts, Sufi poets express their moods and states of being to inspire and encourage, so the reader might ponder the Presence they speak of and move toward personally experiencing that which cannot be expressed in language. As Ain-ol Qhozat Hamadani says "...we speak and write so that things better than talking and writing can come about..."[20] Even in the original language, a poem in this genre is open to personal interpretation based on the individual's receptivity and spiritual ripeness. To quote a Sufi master:

> You must take these poems as mirrors; for you know that a mirror has no form of itself, but rather reflects the face of anyone who looks in it.
> Just so, a poem has no one particular meaning of itself, but presents to each reader his *state of the moment* and the *completeness of his case*....[21]

---

[20]Oseiran, Afif and Alinaqhi Monzavi, editors. *The Letters of Ain-al Qhozat Hamadani*. Tehran, Iran: Asaatir Publications, 1971. In Farsi. Vol-II, 178.
[21]Pourjavady, N. and P. Lambourn. *The Drunken Universe, an Anthology of Persian Sufi Poetry*. New Lebanon, New York: Omega Publications, 1999, 10.

To imagine that one might transmit the intensity and genius in such expressions through translation is rather naïve. Yet, there remains the possibility, however arguable, of rendering the message in another language, i.e., English. In the best of all worlds, a perfect mystic, one whose "case" is complete and whose "state of the moment" is true to the state of eternity, would undertake this project. Until then, works of lesser luminosity, such as the one humbly presented here, will hopefully reflect Jami's message, of the oneness and sanctity of all life.

Note to the Reader

Though I could drink only according to my capacity; in order to try and bring it to you, I had to partake of the wine Jami pours through his verse; and therein lay my reward.

I thank Life and you, my esteemed reader, for occasioning the opportunity of spending hours and hours at the feet of a Naqshbandi Master trying to render his message into English.

May the Wine the Pir[22] offers wash your heart and fill your soul and may the drunkenness He speaks of become your goal, for it is said that with Grace and the Sober One's guidance, we stand a chance of reaching that placeless Abode of Silence where we meet our True Love and our scatteredness ceases.

---

[22]Pir (rhymes with deer): literally an elder, in Sufi lore it refers to One who has completed a certain process which culminates in realizing one's full human potential and experiencing the truth of being cast in God's image. Also referred to as Morshed-e Kaamel (Perfect Master); One who guides others in their struggles for the same realization. The Pir may also be referred to as the Wineseller, the Ancient One, the Sober One, the Elder (Pir) of the Magi and the True One.

My One and Only

O' Final Refuge
container of eternity
accept this failure to praise you
as our praise
                —Nooreddin Ibn-Ahmad-e Jami

1*

Beloved
may I sing the song of your Beauty on these pages
with words that are yours and not mine

to measure You by human imagination
is to try to catch air in a bird cage or water in a fish net
whatever human cleverness might assume You
You are not that and that's all I know

from You comes nothing but blessings
duality runs the workshop that is this place

one out of a thousand blessings we couldn't mention
if in a thousand ways we tried a thousand times

Beloved
our Origin and our Destination
pray accept this inability to praise You
as our praise

ऋ

*References to Farsi sources of all poems are found in the Poem References section at the back of this book.

2

I assumed You outside of myself
beyond the reaches of my imagination
now that You have dropped the veil I realize
You are the One
I left behind with my first step

Cʒ

3

You
who
through this creation
write letters to yourself

You
who
add a thousand new words
on the infinite scroll of this creation
and erase a thousand old ones
every moment

You
whose gorgeous countenance
speaks to the pure of heart
of secrets before the first day of creation
and of eternity's secrets too

You
who on the faces of those who mourn in separation
write stories of remorse
and songs of rapture too

You
who breathe life into meadows and groves
and leave narcissus-faced
and cypress-tall messages for those seeking You

flowers are naught but You
daisies, lilies and roses
are mere poses

all you who read these lines
read them with your heart and not your head
for not his head but Jami's heart has brought them forth

ɷ

4

divulging secrets about your sweet lips
my pen has turned into sugarcane and sugar has covered the
    paper

You are the secret Flame in my broken heart
to turn it into a lantern I'll cover it on all sides with paper

since I know babes are fond of bright colors
I'll let my bleeding heart trace ruby lines on these pages

in the ocean of Love Jami's heart has found many pearls
some of which are offered on these pages

಄

5

in the form of water and dust
none other than You is manifest
in the most secret corner of my heart
and in the depths of my soul
none other than You hides unmanifest

You told me to empty my heart of all that's not You

my world, my heart and soul
who, other than You is in both worlds?
who, other than You
is
in both worlds?

ೞ

6

all beauty is the Beauty of your face
which You command to reflect in your creation
in the eyes of the admirers You then sit
admiring your own reflection

though You are the Beloved,
You don the form of the Lover
and pine for a vision of yourself

You cover your face in your dark tresses
and in that confusion
the entire world You chain to its own speculation

heaven and earth are unable to contain
a speck of your glory
but this tight human chest You have chosen as your territory

you are losing your name and repute in this affair Jami
glory be to you for glorious is the path you've chosen

CB

7

there isn't a particle in creation
that doesn't carry your Light
yesterday I was asking others for a sign of You
today there isn't a sign that isn't of You

03

8

You were always sitting in my eye and I saw You not
in my chest You were hiding and I ran around
searching the whole world I sought a sign of You
the whole world was nothing but You and I saw You not

ဆ

9

a Beauty has stolen my heart but I won't tell who
even if I am beheaded or hanged I still won't tell

the One who has burnt and melted me like a candle
if they set me on fire and burn me head to foot, I won't tell

I am drowning in my tears
but what Pearl I am looking for in these waters I won't tell

here many faces and places come and go in one's mind
but the One who has never left my heart I won't tell

many silver bodied beauties parade in this place
but the One whose Beauty is of the soul I won't tell

fickle-minded and faithless I am being called in this affair
so be it my Darling but everyone knows who that is
even if I don't tell

ଓଃ

10

the Beauty of your countenance no palaces can contain
but this ruin of a heart
You have blessed with your Love

do not deny me the Glory of your face
because of my earthly existence
I have become the veil between us
be generous Love, do away with this veil

this mind is nothing but rust on the mirror of my heart
be generous o Saqhi[23]
let the Wine[24] You bestow
do away with this rust

the Beloved is the Soul of your soul, Jami
no need to traverse the world in search
the Source is within, no need to step outside of your Self

೮೩

---

[23]Saqhi: literally "the cup bearer" in Persian; in Sufi lore it denotes the
Beloved or the Perfect Master.
[24]Wine: in Sufi lore is that Presence who undoes the mind, which
"normally" refuses to be in the present; creating a state of Nonbeing, a
Drunkenness, or Superconsciousness.

11

like the Spring of Eternal Life
hidden in the realm of darkness
the Lord's secret is hidden in this world
a great number of fish appear in the Ocean
the unawake sees the fish and misses the Ocean

଼ଃ

12

in my longing soul and sleepless eye
I am so used to beholding You
that whoever appears at a distance I believe it's You

I am the one crying tears of blood and offering his soul
the One who causes my tears and won't grant me a glance is
    You

You are the Soul of my soul, why should I fear
if my soul is leaving me for You?

how can I complain
if this sorrow ravages me and darkens my days?
for my nights filled with the radiance of your Presence
are the envy of the brightest of days

You say seek no other Jami if you want me as your Friend
no one can be privy to this Love story
my wealth of longing and lack of patience are only known to
    You

being companionless here is a great delight
if one's Friend and Companion is You

ك

13

when humans were molded
Love planted the seed of longing in our clay

You are not of water and soil
but through and through of heart and soul

reveal your Beauty my Beloved and see
how believers and nonbelievers both gather at your door

many set their hearts on promised heavens
for Jami
wherever the Beloved's Presence
there is his Heaven

ଓ

14

how does my heart flutter for You?
like a bird shot through
smeared with its own blood
my heart flutters for You

touch my chest in your generosity
and find out how in your Love
my heart flutters for You

like the heart of a dove in the hunter's grip
except worse
trapped in your tresses my heart flutters for You

like a fish pulled out of water
except worse
in this separation my heart flutters for You

they say their love was one sided
how could that be
when along with Majnoon's heart
Leily's heart fluttered too

Love was the first law in this realm of attractions
Lovers' hearts have always been fluttering for You

be generous and grant Jami a kiss today
for today his heart is so helplessly fluttering for You

ﻼﻼ

15

how can one behold You once
and not cry tears of blood living in separation

though separated from You I exist
I am amazed at anyone who sees Your face once
and separated from You, still exists

છ

16

we name You Wine sometimes
and sometimes we call You the Saqhi
the One who serves the Wine

we see You a trap one moment
and also the One who releases one from the trap

one day we come to know
that on the tablet of life
there is nothing other than your Name
no matter by what name we have called You

೫

17

my heart has again gone to that Beloved who can't be
    described
the One who granted my heart the pain and sorrow which
    can't be expressed

one who is snared by that Glance can't be helped by bravery
for that gorgeous Gazelle is such a fierce Lion that can't be
    described

what matters if outside darkness reigns in blood and tears
if inside there are such visions and lights that can't be
    expressed

your magic whisper is an amazing utterance beyond words
from lips so infinitely refined so impossible to describe

o companions how long will you keep asking Jami who his
    Beloved is
my infinitely delicate Rose is impossible to describe

ଓ

18

it is your light manifest in every atom
a symbol of the unity in all being

though endless and beginningless
You are the beginning and end of all being

from the Wine of Love I desire a cup
and pray, let there be no interference
even from my own being

why should I feel separated from You
when I find your eternal Presence within my own being

in the form of the Beloved we adore You though we know
that in the eyes of the Lovers it is You who sit
and marvel at your own Being

no wayfarer who begins a journey toward You
ever returns to his own land or remembers his own being

a wanderer who spends a moment at your gate
forgets about dusty trails and wonders about his own being

on this path ask for guidance from the Perfect One
who has completed the journey and knows the riddle of being

લ

Of One's True Friend

1

if a word were to be spoken to your heart
about witnessing the Silent Presence here and now
a thousand thoughts would assail your mind
like a thousand flies buzzing around your head

the only chance you have of realizing the Presence
is through the benevolent action of the Pir[25], the Perfect One
in whose company your pesky thoughts are kept at bay
to let your heart taste the Ambrosia left in trust there

rubies are used to charm pythons
the snake that is your ego self can only be charmed by the Pir
seek your way to Master's heart if Understanding is what you
    are after

for one who seeks this Pearl has no choice
but to dare this deepest of Oceans

ɕ

---

[25]See footnote 22.

2

who is the teacher here? Love
and its school? the corner of solitude
no qualifications but unknowing
and my knowing heart is a novice here

no language but silence for this Teacher
alas I know of so few who speak this language
how could one keep the company of the silent
if one's heart is constantly agitated by one's knowing?

the heart which tastes unknowing is submerged in a deluge
    of grace
which washes away all doubts crafted by knowledge and
    cleverness

in the land of devotion
I built a palace made of contentment
speaking less, sleeping less and eating less
are the foundations

inside there is a delightful garden
where flowers and herbs
bring satisfaction to the heart
peace to the mind

everywhere trees, laden with fruits of delight
and the air reverberating with songbirds' songs of praise and
    gratitude

a desert separates the wayfarer from this Paradise
only by giving up hope one may hope to cross this furnace

beware for here bushes offering shade to the weary traveler
have for branches hooks to snare one's soul

none but one who rides a steed with wings of longing
stands a chance here
and when you reach your Destination on such a steed
you will find on its thigh the firebrand of God's own creed

CS

3

the highest activity here is seeking the Pir, the Perfect One
the One who walks in the footsteps of the Pirs of yore
the One compared to whose inner Light
mere reflections are the sun and the moon

the One whose timeless domain is unaffected
by the day's light or the darkness of the night

the One who has left the trap of this existence behind
and rises at will to be one with the One who wears the
    Crown
the Guide whose attraction absorbs you in a domain
outside of all earths, skies, places and domains

but since qualities here bind your soul
you will first need to be released from water and soil
then you will be taken to that placeless Place
below which begins that creation which one may trace

the glory that is the Pir's Presence is the Alchemy
that changes base existence into a practice for Perfection
may Master's Grace be bestowed upon all those
whose hearts in truth yearn for God's Perfection

ભ

4

the turning spheres have brought us spring again
and the new moon promises to usher us into the Wineshop
    again

Nou-rooz[26] has brought the Lovers the gift of a new day and a
    promise
that a new supply of ruby red Wine will be available again

for our new year's present the Friend has given us his word
a word laden with a thousand pledges to restore us to life
    again

the Perfect Master's hand the disciple has been granted
one is protected from calamities when one walks in such
    company
Love's eternal secret the Beloved intended to display
so the nightingale and the rose were granted each other's
    company

ᛒ

---

[26]*Nou-rooz* (literally the new day): the traditional Persian New Year, a
pre-Islamic, Zoroastrian tradition, which places the beginning of the
new year on the first day of Spring. *Nou-rooz* is still very much a living
tradition among Iranians.

5

the naked ones in the garden have awakened
and donned their green robes again

the bird of dawn let out cries of joy this morning
and the garden dwellers have all remembered their chants
    again

the school master and his circle of the learned ran to line up
    at the tavern
to receive Wine from the Pir and their lost hope regain

glory be to those who are so drunk of the moment
as to be released from tomorrows' fears and yesterdays'
    torments

Love can't be mimicked or learned from words, books and
    stories
glory to those who choose silence and are released from all
    allegories

Jami's words reached the songbirds in the meadows
soon they all held their tongues and became all ears

ℭ

6

the self-centered beacon of piety who has made himself a name
knows no principle but gold and no religion but greed

instructed to present himself a knower of spirit's secret
he knows nothing of the beginning, middle or the end

he spends his life winning the hearts of the crowds
and is bitter when he finds his own heart left out

he resents the True Lovers in whose presence all untruth
    cowers
pray watch over my heart Lord so it isn't caught in his
    venomous trap

glory to our Pir in whose tavern of Love
the Holy Spirit empties Blessings cup after cup

our Perfect Friend who has no one's name in his book of
    judgment
and crosses out no one's name in his book of Mercy

ଓଃ

7

my devotion is to my Pir, the Ancient One
whose grace undoes the deeds of the condemned ones

I offer my head for the Wine served in his Tavern
the walls of which stand taller than the heavens

all I can offer him is this threadbare robe of dust
woe to me if He should not accept

whatever our Wineseller does is for our best
judge him not before you fathom his Secret

do not for a moment leave the company of those endowed
    with Christ's breath
for your moments here are counted and they are your true
    wealth

ରଃ

8

pawn all you know in the Tavern and be jolly
mayhap in your old age you can make up for your folly

it is childish to boast of youth's glory and its pleasures
dye your white hair in this Wine and you'll forego all such
    treasures

my heavenly Beauty's Love has drowned me in this bliss
a few more cups of this Wine and from all else I'll find release

in this Love all modesty I have surrendered and am
    scandalized throughout
beware and keep distance all you self-righteous ascetics and
    piously devout

it is ill mannered to come to Love's gate in clever curiosity
from True Lovers one seeks nothing but Love's luminosity

Jami, the Holy Pir is the direction one faces in prayer
whatever one needs on this path one asks that most generous
    Giver

☙

9

for Lovers this world has nothing but torment
and from the worldly crowd only agony one can expect

pilgrims circle structures and seek favors
Lovers are drunk on the Lord and needless of all else

let there be Love in our circle and the Song of Love
to which souls in highest heavens dance and thrive

with the Pir of the Tavern know your manners for at his gate
lions guarding heaven's gates are but dogs bidding his orders

do not stop your Love chants, Jami
for doe-eyed Lovers everywhere relish your songs

ೞ

10

how beautiful it is to be snared by this Beauty
glory be to the bird who is caught in Love's trap

where would I find the courage to behold the Beloved
when at the mere mention of the Name
I forget my entire being

how could Jami ever find his way to the Tavern
were it not for the Grace and Mercy of the Master of Jam[27]

ᑋ

---

[27]Jam: Jami's place of birth in the northeastern region of Khorasan, Iran. Master of Jam refers to Master Kashqhari, the Naqhshbandi Master who initiated Jami into this Sufi order.

11

I knocked on Master's door at dawn
asking for a respite from my meaningless existence

that can't be for as long as you are guileful, He said
and put my guile to rest with a cup of Wine

may my life be an offering at his feet
for without the Light on his face
no lost wayfarer stands a chance

here, where king and pauper are confined to a pile of dust
of what use is pomp and circumstance
those who seek to pick from the tree of salvation
need from all else to wash their hands

ରୁ

Of You
and Me

1

Beloved
no fear if You break my heart a thousand times
but do not abandon me in contempt because of what I have
here become
for in this garden every flower has its roots in dirt

ॐ

2

after it had been nourished by the waters of ancient rains
the reed raised its head
it beheld itself and saw that it was encased in a robe of cane

next it beheld the mud out of which it had appeared
and knew then that it was tied by many knots to where it had
    taken birth

o Friend
the reed moaned
lend me a hand
so I may move away from this mud

time passed and when it was right the Flute Player appeared
He removed the many layers of cane and undid the reed's
    many knots
the reed was now smooth outside and empty inside
He then put the reed to his lips and finding it empty of itself
breathed in the selfless reed all his secrets in the form of
    melodies

the reed declared then that it was no more
and it was right for now it was a flute

his breath is in me and my voice is his tune, the reed
    announced humbly
I am him and He is me though to the ignorant this be
    blasphemy

You have gone far enough Jami and should stop now for you
    well know
that in the circle of Lovers there is a covenant
that neither the tongue nor the pen may reveal the Secret
everyone knows that it was for such revelations
that the one who declared *anal-haq*[28] was sent to the
    oppressor's gallows

ꙅ

---

[28] *Anal-haq*: "I am the truth" was declared by Hosein-ebne-Mausoure
Hallaj, a Mystic born in the southwestern province of Fars in Iran. Not
surprisingly he was accused of heresy by the established clergy. Hosein
was also a relentless and outspoken critic of the excesses of the corrupt
Abbassids who ruled the vast domains of the Muslim empire of the
day. In 922 he was executed in Baghdad immediately becoming the
most celebrated Sufi martyr in history.

3

one who harbors no longing for his Origin
of human heritage he has received a form only
the rest is missing
Life bestows a cure for every pain
but for painlessness no cure can be found

൯

4

lucky is the one who realizes the secret of being nobody
for no one gets anywhere by being somebody

whatever is not about desirelessness and detachment
is a delusion and will but lead to disillusion

there is a light on your face
which whispers of the Divine Flame
as God is my witness you have issued from the same

for the caged bird to reach the perfumed garden
it has to pass through the realm of imagination

you have to rise above that
which you think human destiny
to fulfill your destiny
for your covenant is not with man
but with God

should you be not allowed yet
to join the Beloved's caravan
be content if you hear its bells from a distance

in the realm of hearts none but our King rules
the One who by day is the Ruler
and by night the Life bestowing Thief!

∞

5

when the dawn comes
be of the early risers
during the day be of the mourners
cling to the One who cannot leave you
and from all else wash your hands

ೞ

6

you are Love's creation
look nowhere else for sustenance
turn to Love

lover and beloved
Master and disciple
are naught but Love

keep out the illusion of duality
do not breach the covenant of Unity

detachment is a fortress of light
in Love's eye counts no other light

one who has not been bestowed with the gift of Love
his vision no one may trust

Jami came from the Beloved
and dissolved back in Him
from the Beloved is our origin
and it is our destiny to return to Him

ᛋ

7

I am bewildered and cannot fathom
the attraction of the soul to the body
this bright light trapped in this prison of dark mud

for a lifetime I have struggled with a thousand me's
I am still confounded and can't figure out what this me
    means

℀

8

from the inner sanctum of Union I was cast out
fancy where I have been, pity where I have ended up

free from mind's treachery my soul was blissful in my
    Beloved's company
once I began with hows and whys I had to endure
    separation's tyranny

agreements and disagreements I was spared in your company
I agreed to a single request and landed myself in this infamy

the origin of all sound is your life-bestowing Breath, Beloved
from that Original Sound I was separated as a melody

deprived of Life and thirsting for Love I searched
till I beheld your Beauty and, blissfully content, I drowned

now I know that there is no place where You are not
and that it was your desire
that I land in this place of wants and desires

I am nothing but a cup fashioned to serve Love's Wine
rescue me with a cupful o' Saqhi
so I don't remain empty

ᛦ

47

9

you are destined to fly across worlds
do not soil your royal wings in this mud pit

trapped in this body and pulled by its weight
soul from body you can't tell and your essence you neglect

you busy yourself looking for happiness in this dust bin
and your true home in the highest skies you can't imagine

you seek refuge in wealth and glory in steadfast illusion
what perfect ignorance, what baffling delusion

છ

10

do not fret over your daily existence here
you are not less than the bird who trusts and is sustained

the worldly one's heart is so blind by greed
that though he daily sees someone buried
to his own death he pays no heed
behind colorful robes our sire hides and acts gruff
till such time that death arrives and calls his bluff

from dervish's solitude the sultan is shut out
for the bird of Intimacy is too delicate, and the sultan, too
    crude

if you are a wayfarer on this path
know that reining in your desires is wiser
than sitting on King Solomon's throne and reigning in his
    domains

in your heart plant a sapling from the tree of contentment
nourish it with watchful vigilance for in time a tree will grow
the fruits of which will keep you eternally content

ରଓ

11

when an unfortunate is not wanted near the Beloved's Throne
to the disease of insatiable greed he is made prone
his nights and days he spends collecting material
right and wrong for him remain immaterial
no crime is a crime and no low is too low
and then a troupe of blind cheerleaders is provided
to hail his crimes as success and call the wretch a hero

⌘

12

this world and all in it is a rotting corpse
and the worldly are here for their piece of flesh

a single true human being you won't find among them
though you may go through them a thousand times

when the dawn comes be of the early risers
during the day keep aloof
better be as lowly as the dust on the road
despised and rejected by everyone
than to be a pompous pretender
revered by seventy-two nations' fools

ೞ

13

ignorance has blocked our sire's mind so entirely
that though he continually witnesses
those near and dear die and disappear
he never ponders his own final affair

covered in fineries he has figured out the riddle of life
and lives in denial of the day when death calls our bluff

03

14

do not pain yourself over treasures buried in dirt
gain needlessness and let dirt keep its treasures

riches and glory in this realm are not worth the price
few kings keep their throne in this game of dice

heed the crow and the owl who have taken over
the delightful terraces and castles of kings of yore

you need to escape for a day or two from senses and places
for the solution to your dilemma is outside of appearances

not much time before autumn crashes through the gates
though neither the rose will pay heed nor the jasmine
Jami, one's affliction here comes of one's own deeds
no use blaming destiny or accusing stars and heavens of
tyranny

ಔ

15

nothing here but pettiness, cunning and degradation
we are all sinking in sorrow on this wave of existence
would that our ship had not found its way
from the ocean of Oneness to this coast of scatteredness

ന

16

whatever you may find here
life or death will soon steal it from you
surrender your heart to the One who
in different forms of being
has and will always be with you

೫

17

to the wise this place and all in it is worth nothing
joys and sorrows here only enslave you

strengthen your will to find release from this prison
for your will is the ladder to help you across the prison wall

do not break anyone's heart here
for that crystal bowl is easy to break and impossible to mend

Jami do not do unto others what you wouldn't like to be done
    unto you
alas too many are the clever and so this advice is popular with
    too few

ॐ

18

do not become attached to what life gives you here
for in time you will give it to someone
to hold your hand
or to some dog
to let go of your foot

 CB

19

you who carry a thousand grudges in your heart
release your heart from faces and places
and your grudges will be lost
in the flea market of this life
all you may hope to find is confusion
center your heart on the One
and be spared this scatteredness

ೞ

20

may your heart be illumined by the Giver of Light

may it be trusted with Eternity's Secret

may you triumph over all domains
without moving a finger

ය

The Divine Music

1

though the entire creation is filled with this Melody
the unawake can hear It not

glory, glory, glory to the Musician to whose Tune
every ecstatic particle in creation dances accordingly

the lyre and the lute are declaring in adoration
You are the Cause, Beloved, You are Perfection
the Lover is drowned in this boundless Ocean
the clever preacher vies for a place on the shore of delusion

Love's Creator wears no manifest face
yet on every face nothing but That is manifest
in Leily's garb Love appears to Majnoon
steals his patience and brings him sweet doom

in truth Love is always loving Herself
Leily and Majnoon are but stage names

Jami saw the Cup Bearer's face reflected in the goblet once
and like the pitcher has not stopped bowing to the goblet since

ଔ

2

glory to the Musician whose Melody
erases everything that burdens the heart
the One whose breath blowing in the flute
releases us from all that burdens our mind

for lifetimes the clever mind was building castles in the air
a wave from the Ocean of Love rose
and all thoughts have disappeared in its roar

my heart was given a taste of Love's Sorrow
and in its longing it has found release from all joys and sorrows
my laments I'd bring You, my Beloved, and complain
but whenever I behold You neither my complaints nor I remain

lend no ear to the hunchback who rules here
for he is given to only one pleasure
to rob you of your Love, your True Treasure

drink this Wine and relish your ecstasy in solitude
for it's the only way out of this place of servitude

Jami learned to worship this Wine at the Pir's gate
whoever apprentices with the Master learns his trait

 C3

3

if from all idle noise your mind's ear be emptied
the beating of the drums and singing of the lute you will hear

more of this ruby Wine o Cupbearer then we shall see
about this place of deeds and consequences

for the bird of heavens trapped in this domain
nothing is more desirable than this heavenly Wine

if our Pir hasn't emptied a cup in his solitude
what is this drunken glow in his eyes and this gratitude

spare me stories of the preacher's miracles and his devotion
the glow in your eyes tells your true story and the rest is fiction

Beloved, in the beginning there was only You and so shall it
    be at the end
in between, claims to existence are illusions and sooner or later
    shall but end

 C03

4

the celestial harp sings of Love's Secrets in your gatherings
and the lute whispers of the ecstasy of your Presence

of what use would my existence be
if your Beauty I weren't called upon to witness

You mete out what's for each one of us
for You hold the brush that paints all existence

Your face is the Sun of the inner skies
the most exquisite Light in the realm of lights

undo the veil Beloved so the one who refused to bow to Adam[29]
would joyfully prostrate at your gate in repentance

let in both worlds this be Jami's honor
that to his Beloved's gate he brought his Love and nothing else

ೞ

---

[29]In Sufi lore it is said that when Adam was created, the Lord asked
the heavenly host to bow to him. Satan refused, saying he reserved that
honor only for his Beloved Lord and that no creature made of "clay"
deserved it. He vowed to prove that humans cannot appreciate that
inner Essence, who is of God; that we are slaves to our animal
instincts, and that self-preservation is all we know. This battle, it is
said, is waged within every human being, Satan does everything to
turn one's face away from one's true Essence, from God, and keep the
individual within that lonely, isolated bubble made of one's delusional,
self-centered view of life.

5

whoever is lucky to smell the fragrance of your Wineshop
lives drunk on Love for as long as he lives
and dies in ecstasy when he dies

your Love is the body of which I am the shadow
I run when You run and walk when You walk

how can the lover not cry tears of blood
when the Beloved is distant, no road is in sight
and the Guide is so hard to find

no matter who the company and what the occasion
my heart and soul abandon the scene and run to You for
    consolation

Jami needs no musicians or bards for in his chest's cavity
he hears the Celestial Song of Love's Sweet Captivity

ᴄ༄

Of Love

1

learn the secret of spiritual poverty from that Love Derelict,
    the Rend[30]
who has surrendered his all for the Wine served in Love's
    Tavern

                                ଓ

---

[30] *Rend*: literally a rascal; in Sufi lore a *rend* is one with no respect for
outer appearances and conventions, one entirely given to inner mean-
ing, with no regard for worldly gain or loss.

2

away from You
I am fed up with my existence, Friend
I can bear being away from all and everyone
separation from you is beyond me, Friend

whenever we come together
I want to read You my book of sorrows
but long before I get near there
I loose my speech, Friend

You ask how my heart feels
how could I know anything about my heart
it has for so long been sitting at your feet, Friend

do not send me away
for all I wish to do with my life
is to offer that too at Your feet, Friend

ೞ

3

last night my moans set the heavens on fire
angels fluttered with burnt wings like moths set aflame

how could sleep touch me in that agony
when my bedding was on fire and my pillow flooded with tears

the ascetic's lips are parched and the Sufi's eyes are flooded
woe to those caught in this Love for it burns both the wet
    and the dry

whoever is torched here by this Fire becomes luminous
and attracts a hundred others and sets them too on Fire

the dull theologian preaches aloofness and denies Love
may he and his congregation both burn in Love's Fire

Jami imagined speaking of this affair in a poem
flames issued from his pen and set his whole house on Fire

                        ℘

4

Love
You have attained a thousand faces and then some
everything we may imagine You are that and then some
seventy-two nations have sung your praises
You are all those songs
and then some

ॐ

5

Love has taught my days the ways of the night
brought my heart patience and my soul warmth

do not blame my eyes for shedding tears
dropping Love pearls they learned from your mouth

I know no religion higher or happier than Love
blessed is the wayfarer who finds his way to this Grove

o' keeper of records wash away Lovers' records
for Love was long before tablets and records

since the day he heard Love's whisper in his Essence
Jami has cared for nothing but that pure Presence

൫

6

a hundred streams of joy emptied into my life
finding my heart empty of Love
they turned into tears of longing
and left through my eyes

he boasted of his courage and chivalry
when Jami first braved this circle of Longing
thus and here he is learning of his need and his wanting

ひ

7

all else has left this heart, only the Beloved's face remains
all smoke has cleared out, the Flame only remains

every desire has been erased in the True One's company
except the desire for more of the Wine served in that company

in Leily's love Majnoon roamed the burning desert and
    became a legend
his bitter sufferings lovers recount as a sweet legend

Jami was possessed of piety, patience and both this world and
    the next
glory to Love who rid him of all his possessions and released
    him
from both this world and the next

ം

8

other than this sweet pain of Love all is vain
vanities here distract one from true gain

beauty was what I searched for in everyone and everything
now that I have seen You, all other gain is but pain

I am all tears and anticipation now
and though your company I am denied in this affliction
when this is done and I am no more
my dust will blow only in your direction

many poems Jami offers at your gate
and they all and always only state
You are all I want
all else is a mistake

ଓ

9

my Darling's name I do not know
who may I ask?
the One who has taken possession of my heart
I need to know who but do not know whom to ask

a hundred elegant words I line up to present my story
when that Enchanter appears I forget myself and my story
have mercy and show me the way to that Sweet Thief
my heart is foregone, my life too I will offer for a vision,
    however brief

my sighs and longing I send that Darling on the breeze of dawn
glory to the day when I may live in that Presence released from
    dusks and dawns

pray, my Lord, when I am no more, from my dust and this Love
fashion a bird so I may ask birds of heaven the way to my
    Beloved's grove

               ❧

10

drop all coverings and bring along your lovesick heart
then you may walk in Love's company
be erased from your own being and surrender
shadowlessly walk in Love's company
better to willingly choose to be dust in this Love
for eventually there'll be no choice, only dust

ᘓ

11

I will speak to you openly of my Beloved
everything comes from Him and if you keenly observe
everything is the Beloved

every particle in creation reflects our Darling's face
the veil in between is our hopes and regrets

why pray in a direction determined by another
when in every direction you look there is no one but the
    Beloved?

from Him comes all good and all evil and yet
evil is evil with us
from the Beloved is issued only good

in this place of scatteredness my heart is in many pieces
but this longing brings hopes of Union and Oneness

worry not, Jami, speaking of Union so boldly
for drunken Lovers' trespasses our Beloved forgives kindly

08

12

every strand of hair in your tresses
ropes in the ecstatic Lover

Lovers' seeking would lead nowhere
were it not for the Beloved's pull within

⦋

13

I swear by God that in all the worlds nothing but God is
life's Secret is nameless and placeless
names and places count for nothing

long have you followed the blind and their stories and theories
it's time to search your way to the realm of certainties
for theories and stories count for nothing

your fears and hopes are mists to hide from you your Beloved
till you realize in certainty that aside from your True Desire
all else, here or elsewhere, counts for nothing

your renunciation and philanthropy you barter for the crowd's
    attention
how will this please you in that Solitude
where crowds and their adoration count for nothing?

o preacher if you burn in this Love then warm our souls and
    lend us Light
otherwise remain quiet
for here loud gestures and verses learned in school count for
    nothing

surrender your tongue, reveal not your Secret
for in the realm of Silence, what the tongue can reveal
can only count for nothing

if you are a slave to Love then leave name and lineage behind
for in Love's circle so and so son of so and so
counts for nothing

ᥩ

14

when I open my mouth to speak, your Name is all I utter
this cannot be helped, for my Darling's name is all I remember

if I receive a hundred wounds I dare not moan
for my delicate Beloved cannot stand complaints

I threw myself at Love's feet and asked for justice
"rise Jami," I was told, "in the religion of Love, there's no
     justice"

 C8

15

hear the story of our Beloved from the Beloved
or from One who has heard it from the Beloved

beyond all attributes is that Darling
among the Lovers this is the attribute of the Beloved

Love's language is needless of words and speech
all speech is an effort to translate that language

whenever a rose appears in any garden
love birds offer their song to the rose
but their true praise is for the Beloved

for as long as I have to carry a head on my shoulders
may it lay in the dust at the gate of my Beloved

do not look to hear such truths from the pulpit, Jami
only the Sincere are allowed the secrets of the Beloved

૭૪

16

in this Love, my heart has become needless of my body
and heedless of my mind
devoted entirely to the Beloved
it has been released from the world and worldly worry

untouched by time and space are You and yet
neither time nor space is without You

doubts and certainties are both distractions here
glory be to the one who in this Love
has left doubts and certainties both behind

ask me not about gains and losses
for in this Love I am heedless of losses
and needless of gains

my tongue is busy repeating your name
and my heart is occupied with your dream
my heart is full and my tongue is never idle

Beloved, slay me in Love's name
for thus is one released from all desire

Love affords relief from mind's treachery, Jami
never lose sight of the Lovers' company

ॐ

17

intellect was lecturing that the Beloved is such and thus
Love whispered that Infinity is free of such and thus

it is Love's way to reveal the Truth
mind too is revealed to itself by Love

near and far, everyone is drunk of this Love
kings and paupers both are nobodys in this Love

the desert that separates Majnoon from Leily is not crossed
before Majnoon becomes Leily and Leily turns into Majnoon

Jami, speak of the Beloved only, for in the Lovers' midst
all other subjects are tall tales and myths

കൃ

18

Jami, let go of contrivances, loud prayer beads and appearances
the Darling you are after is too clever for such pretenses

the self-centered theologian is too absorbed in his own designs
to be able to behold the Naqshband,[31] the true Maker of all
designs

our exalted sire is too full of himself and bitter bile
parched he will go to the grave, though he live on the river Nile

to our preacher appearance and grooming have become religious
hallmarks
he deserves to be laughed at by the stalwart Rend[32] for his ges-
tures and remarks

the insincere will hear no response from heavens
though they may crack the ceiling of the temple with their loud
incantations

---

[31]Naqshband: "Maker of designs" (Farsi) a play on the word
Naqshbandi, the Sufi brotherhood initiated by Sheikh Baha-oddin
Naqshband (1318-1389) who was born in Qasr-e Arefoon near
Bokhara in present day Uzbekistan; the area was generally referred to
as Mavara-ol-Nahr, meaning the region north of the river Oxus, or
Transoxania. Also see, Afsahzad, Ala Khan. *A Critical Study of Jami's
Biography and Writings*. Under the supervision of the Written Heritage
Publication Office, Center for Iranian Studies, Tehran, 1999.
[32]See Footnote 30, page 71.

one who avoids the Perfect Human's[33] company neglects human
   heritage
and will never be able to even imagine Khezr[34]
let alone walk in His company

☙

---

[33]The Perfect Human: refers to those who have completed their spiritu-
al journey and having realized their full human potential, are estab-
lished in their Essence, who is "God".
[34]Khezr (Khidr-Arabic): literally a green, living plant. In Sufi lore it
refers to an archetypal, mythic guide, the eternal prophet, the Green
Archangel who knows the secret of eternal life. It may also refer to the
Perfect Master.

19

whose tipsy eyes have caused this drunkenness in me?
whose bow has delivered this arrow in my heart?

Lovers relish suffering as gifts from the Friend
ask not why and how but who
it all comes from

ෆ

20

Love's religion is selflessness
nothing but longing and detachment is allowed here

all magic is but deception
Love's the Magic that grants vision

willingly accept whatever is given to you
for in Love's court, being offended is the worst offense

whys and hows are not welcome here
to Lovers the idle curious are the wrong company

ରଃ

Of Wine and the Tavern

1

o Saqhi pass the cup of Wine
and be generous with mine
I am hopelessly stuck with me
pray release me for a spell from me

I wish to be seen by no eyes
glory to the moment when
in Love's glorious mist
I am covered even from my own eyes

between You and me
there is no veil but me
come
be generous and let this veil be undone

reveal that Glory my Friend
which ushers one to that Nonexistence
where existence finds Life

there can be no sign of eternal life for you
until Love has erased all your signs
and cleansed you of all yous

Love's domain is not in places and regions
come Jami, show us a way out of regions and places

 C8

2

a hundred years of prayers won't merit a sip of this Wine
but how can this secret be given to one who has tasted only
   grape wine?

Beloved
your eyes bewitch steadfast ascetics in their solitude
who ever saw a gazelle hunting fierce lions?

any heart to which You find your way
becomes a burning star and glows forever
seven heavens will burn to ashes
if a single sigh were to escape a Lover's heart

had the preacher tasted your lips
heaven's milk and honey he wouldn't hawk

like the ant who stores the season's harvest under the ground
Jami will carry his dreams of uniting with You to his grave

☙

3

in spring I pawn my robe to pay for my Wine
let the pious consider my manners amiss
You are that Beauty from whom the sun borrows its glory
I would pawn my very soul in your shop for a kiss

lifetimes I have spent pining at your door
and though I am about to expire
my heart is still on fire

fickleness is your way
woe to him who falls for You
I have become the laughing stock of the children
such deserves an elder who harbors dreams of union with
    Eternal Youth

Jami pawned his rosary and cloak in the Master's Tavern
to be drunk on this Wine and to join the circle of Lovers

෬

4

I was in the Tavern drinking of this Wine
when there was no sign of grape nor of grape vine

ask not for signs from those gathered in the Wineshop
long before one gets there one has given up all signs

when you turn to dust, o heart, settle on the road to the
    Wineshop
where our drunken Darling may pass in revelry and spill a drop

glory to that Friend who comforting those burning in their
    adoration
goes house to house hiding that Glory which no one could
    behold
and live in obedience through this separation

every beauty here is a reflection of some quality
of which the Soul of our soul is the sum totality

Love is not mimicked o preacher
one has to taste It
before one offers It

drop this pretentious cloak of abstention, Jami
for our Beloved keeps the meek's and the Rend's[35] company

CR

---

[35]Rend: see footnote 30, page 71.

5

for those caught by anxiety
in times of chaos and ill humor
no cure is more effective than our Wine
another cup o Saqhi for we have been discovered
and the bitter inquisitor is mightily upset at our circle divine

it is futile to look for your True Friend elsewhere
empty your heart of all and you'll find him right there

cut down on your sleep to bring your Beloved into your
    dreams
for this great boon is granted in early dawn to the sleepless
    dreamer
learn to keep your Love's Secret yours
it was for revealing his that Mansour[36] walked up the cruel
    gallows

Jami, value your pearls brought up from the ocean of solitude
do not offer them to the self absorbed for they are not worthy

ભ

---

[36]Mansour referring to Hosein-ibn-e Mansour Hallaj, see *Anal-haq*,
footnote 28, page 41.

Jami
the Man
the Poet
the Mystic

1

I wish I could know who I am
and what my wanderings here are for

if assured of the Beloved's approval
I would make merry and sing heartily
if not
I would borrow a thousand eyes to weep with

☙

2

*Selected sections from a eulogy written by Jami at his teenaged son
Safee-eddin's death:*

in this ancient garden where on the same vine thorns and
  roses grow
you will not find a heart that has not been broken and run
  through

do not look for comfort here and seek no rest
for restlessness runs this shop and sorrows put you to test

from the slain deer's gland comes perfumed musk
the scent of blood and sorrow of death carry it must

do not pick up the sleeping lute and playfully strum it
unless you are ready for a hundred sorrowful tunes hiding in it

see how cruel destiny has cheated me
and of all forbearance and patience it has robbed me

෨

a thousand pearls stream down my face every minute
since my pearl, my Safee-eddin, was stolen from me

the prettiest spring blossom in my garden of joy
was cut in its prime to decorate the heavenly garden

o heart, fly with my sighs and lift to heavens fair

bring my laments and whisper my sorrows in Safee-eddin's ear

the earth swallowed you for a tiny morsel
when you had had so few morsels on this earth

how could you leave with tears of blood streaming down my
    face
daddy's sweet life, how could you not pity daddy's wretched
    soul?

a hundred times I would have torn my heart out
were my actions not to put to question my faith

he would give his and have your life returned
if daddy thought the Giver of life would heed his thoughts

෨

like Jacob I am losing my sight to grief
send me your scent and restore my vision my sweet Joseph[37]

---

[37]Joseph was the beloved son of Jacob (Old Testament); he was sold to
slavery by his jealous brothers who told their father that Joseph had
been killed. Grief drove Jacob blind. Years later, Joseph, who had
become the beloved of Egypt because of his purity and virtue, sent his
shirt to his father, and Jacob was healed and gained his sight back by
smelling the shirt.

I can ask no one about your welfare there
but I may console myself talking to your memory here

under this cold mud how are you faring?
without you here we are drowned in tears
without anyone there, how are you faring?

we are falling apart without you here
and that's how we are in each other's company
how are you faring in your lonely solitude there?

I am standing at your grave
you who were your father's crown
now under everyone's feet, how are you faring?

without you, life on earth has become a punishment for me
you who took your abode underground, how are you faring?

෩

you turned your face away from this place of existence
and flew towards planes of nonexistence
I am tired of this place, on those planes, how are you faring?

withering away, I am consumed by this pain
alas, you won't even in my dreams ask me how I'm faring?

though your separation drowned my soul and turned my
  heart heavy
lightheartedly you sprang out of this whirlpool and deserve to
  be merry

you came pure and pure you returned to the invisible domain
lucky is the beautiful canary who leaves the land of the deaf
  and blind in a hurry

here one can't but contemplate one's own death
and ponder one's sojourn when others complete theirs

ଛ

everyone and everything in this deceitful domain is but
  another trap
nothing but annihilation in the Real saves one here

become dust, and remain dust, for at the end
these turning spheres grind and scatter your dust

become forgetful of your self and you will gain freedom
before time eliminates you from its kingdom

Jami, surrender and leave behind whatever is not the Truth
withdraw from the rest and ponder this in solitude

ଓଷ

3

o tulip, you have just risen from the ground
tell me
have you any news from that rose
who recently fell in the dust?

కఠ

4

no more interested in loud merriments and revelry
no more desires but to be in undisturbed solitary

as a caged bird longing to circle Love's abode in heaven
my trapped soul has no other fetters than this tattered body

I count my shortcomings on my prayer beads
precious little else remains within reach

other than the desire to leave occasional traces in verse
I desire no other disruptions in my midsummer day's
    dreamless rest

my self-willed existence has finally departed
and has left me a wealth of spiritual poverty
I am desireless of everything and everyone
though I still thirst for that Hallowed Secret that is the spirit's
    True Poverty

ଔ

5

we had to surrender our hope and let the Friend go
we had to taste separation after union and let the Friend go

companionless, forlorn and left behind
we had to surrender to His wish and let the Friend go

all night floating upside down or sideways
we turned around that abode but gained no entrance
unable to kiss his hand
we kissed the guardian's feet at the gate and let the Friend go

no longer fettered by pride
we rubbed our face in the dust in His lane and let the Friend go

since the treasure of His company was not destined
we gazed at the windows of His abode and let the Friend go

Love's pain has grabbed Jami by the throat
we have washed our hands of him and soon, him too, we'll
    let go

CB

6

neither a sweetheart
whose love warms my heart and delights my evening
whose wishes are my commands
and whose bright countenance lights up my dark night
nor a most trustworthy friend
whose refinement and sincerity
brings joy to one's heart and dispels perplexity
nor even a soul companion who may enter any moment
and chase sorrows and usher in merriment

can match that elation and highest gratitude
that comes from single pointed collection of one's attention
in solitude

o Jami, when the bitterness of loneliness assails
find solace in poetry written in such fashion

ଔ

7

the soul that travels between the realm of its Beloved and this
    body
becomes a bird of sorrow who flies in realms dreams dare not
    reach
only to return to a dusty cage it cannot breach

for one such as me, boasting of your Love can only bring
    shame
in a place of arrivals and departures claims to steadfastness are
    vain
but, for as long as I live, with every breath I will draw in
    your Name

counting his breaths and eyeing the door of the body's cage
away from You
Jami's soul only waits for her pilgrimage

 C3

8

if I should lose a hundred souls to reach the Soul of my soul,
    so be it
whatever that Darling wishes and desires, so be it

should the Beloved's heart my moans soften a little
I will have my way with her heart little by little

for this malady no one has offered a cure on earth
one can only beg for mercy from heavens

no friend or ally can be true in this domain
better be friends with the dogs guarding the Beloved's domain

there is no pleasure for the tongue higher than telling this
    Love story
for as long as I can move my tongue I will recount this story

so long has Jami spoken of the Beloved's sweet lips that he
    deserves to be remembered
as a sweet loving, sweet tongued, wily parrot

ଓଃ

9

I am in Love but won't tell you who

I am delirious but know not why

I am drunk of that Wine which is needless of goblets
in Love with that Darling who lives in the placeless place
glory to this Wine a sip of which
has stolen me from myself
another cup o Saqhi
and I will be lost to all thoughts of loss
and dead to the thought of death

then
when I am dead to death
I will rise in the realm of Eternity

and
I will play the game of Love with You, my Beloved
with no mind for other than You

then
I will vanish altogether into Jami's truth
and Truth will declare
You are all
there is
was
and ever will be

ය

POEM REFERENCES

Poems in each section are indexed by number, page and volume, according to the annotation in the original Farsi version: Afsahzad, Ala Khan, editor. *Divan Jami* (Nur al-Din Abdal-Rahman ibn Ahmad Jami). Under the supervision of the Written Heritage Publication Office, Center for Iranian Studies, Tehran, 1999. Vol I: Fatehat al-shabab Vol II & III: Wasetat al-eqd and Katemat al-hayat.

Dedication: no. 232 / p. 336 / bk.-I
Epigraph: Adham, p. 878 / bk.-III
    no. 45, p. 857, bk.-I

Part I: One and Only

1...no. 1 / p. 41 / bk.-I
2...no. 14 / p. 851 / bk.-I
3...no. 434 / p. 354 / bk.-II
4...no. 167 / p. 576 / bk.-III
5...no. 12 / p. 851 / bk.-I
6...no. 896 / p. 766 / bk.-I
7...no. 10 / p. 850 / bk.-I
8...no. 77 / p. 864 / bk.-I
9...no. 176 / p. 301 / bk.-I
10...no. 451 / p. 364 / bk.-II
11...no. 98 / p. 867 / bk.-I

12...no. 1005 / p. 833 / bk.-I
13...no. 12 / p. 250 / bk.-I
14...no. 570 / p. 558/ bk.-I
15...no. 27 / p. 854 / bk.-I
16...no. 3 / p. 849 / bk.-I
17...no. 774 / p. 691 / bk.-I
18...no. 247 / p. 230 / bk.-II

Part II: Of One's True Friend

1...no. 6/ p. 56 / bk.-I select
2...no. 6 / p. 56 / bk.-I
3...no. 8 / p. 77 / bk.-I
4...no. 74 / p. 515 / bk.-III
5...no. 123 / p. 548 / bk.-III
6...no. 483 / p. 501/ bk.-I
7...no. 477 / p.497 / bk.-I
8...no. 752 / p. 676 / bk.-I
9...no. 147 / p. 166 / bk.-II
10...no. 384 / p. 436 / bk.-I
11...no. 259 / p. 636 / bk.-III

Part III: Of You and Me

1...no. 197 / p. 314 / bk.-I
2...no. 305 / p. 269 / bk.-II
3...no. 6 / p. 56 / bk.-1 select
4...no. 455 / p. 366 / bk.-II
5...no. 61 / p. 860 / bk.-I
6...no. 144 / p. 164 / bk.-II
7...no. 133 / p. 874 / bk.-I
8...no. 365 / p. 308 / bk.-II
9...lines 591-595 / p. 95 / bk.-I
10...selected from no. 6 / p. 56 / bk.-I
11...no. 5 / p. 662 / bk.-III
12...no. 7 / p. 662 / bk.- III
13...lines 227-8 / p. 61 / bk.-I
14...no. 247 / p. 346 / bk.-I

Part VI: Of Wine and the Tavern

1...no. 31 / p. 92 / bk.-II
2...no. 382 / p. 435 / bk.-I
3...no. 265 / p. 640 / bk.-III
4...no. 719 / p. 654 / bk.-I
5...no. 168 / p. 180 / bk.-II

Part VII: Jami, the Man, the Poet, the Mystic

1...no. 154 / p. 977 / bk.-I
2...no. 164-169 / vol. I- selected
3...no. 73 / p. 868 / bk.-I
4...no. 155 / p. 567 / bk.-III
5...no. 221 / p. 329 / bk.-I
6...no. 348 / p. 297 / bk.-II
7...no. 136 / p. 557 / bk.-III
8...no. 173 / p. 184 / bk.-II
9...no. 4 / p. 467/ bk.-III

BIBLIOGRAPHY

Abramian, Vraje, translator. *Nobody Son of Nobody: Poems of Sheikh Abu-Saeed Abil-Kheir*. Prescott, Arizona: Hohm Press, 2001.

Afsahzad, Ala Khan, editor. *Divan Jami* (Nur al-Din Abdal-Rahman ibn Ahmad Jami) Under the supervision of the Written Heritage Publication Office, Center for Iranian Studies, Tehran, 1999. Vol I: Fatehat al-shabab Vol II & III: Wasetat al-eqd and Katemat al-hayat.

Afsahzad, Ala Khan. *A Critical Study of Jami's Biography and Writings*. Under the supervision of the Written Heritage Publication Office, Center for Iranian Studies, Tehran, 1999.

Beny, Roloff. *Persia, Bridge of Turquoise*. Foreword by Seyyed Hossein Nasr. Toronto, Canada: The Canadian Publishers, McClelland and Stewart, Limited, 1975. Printed and bound in Italy by Arnoldo Mondadori Editore, Verona.

Davis, F. Hadland. *The Persian Mystics*. London, John Murray, 1908. Wisdom of the East Series.

de Nicholas, Antonio T. *Saint John of the Cross, Alchemist of the Soul: His Life His Poetry (Bilingual) His Prose*. New York: Paragon House, 1989. Text, New Edited Translations by Antonio T. de Nicholas. Foreword by Seyyed Hossein Nasr. *Not for All the Beauty*, pp. 147-151; *By the Waters of Babylon, Psalm* 136 pp. 76-81; *Not Living in Myself I Live*, pp. 139-142; *Dark Night*, pp. 103-105.

Heravi, Najib Mayel. *Sheikh Abdorrahman Jami*. Tehran, Iran: Tarh-e No Publications, 1998. In Farsi. Quotations from pp. 35, 36 and 38.

Hosein Badreddin, Mohammad Mansoor ibn-e Abi-Saeed. *Asrarottohid fi maqhamat Sheikh Abu-Saeed ibn-e Abil Kheir.* Tehran, Iran, 1972. In Farsi.

Isfahani, Seyyed Ahmad Hatef. *Divan-e Hatef Isfanhani.* Tehran, Iran: Negah Publications, 1969. In Farsi. Based on Vahid Dastgerdi's corrected version, Introduction/Biography by Abbas Eqbal Ashtiani.

Jami, Hakim Nuruddin Abdurrahman. (David Pendlebury, translator.) *Yusuf and Zulaikha: An Allegorical Romance.* London: Octagon Press for the Sufi Trust, 1980.

Lewisohn, Leonard, editor. *Classical Persian Sufism: From Its Origins to Rumi.* London: Khaniqahi Nimatullahi Publications, 1993. Foreword: Dr. J. Noorbakhsh; Introduction: S. H. Nasr.

Mason, Herbert. "Hallaj and the Bagdad School of Sufism." In: *Classical Persian Sufism: From Its origins to Rumi.* (Leonard Lewisohn, editor), London: Khaniqahi Nimatullahi Publications, 1993. pp. 65-81.

Matt, Daniel C. *The Essential Kabbalah: The Heart of Jewish Mysticism.* Edison, New Jersey: Castle Books, 1997.

Mohtasham, Dr. Nasrin (Khazai). *Works of Fakhreddin Eraqi.* Tehran, Iran: Zavvar Publications, 1966. In Farsi.

Moyne, John and Coleman Barks. *Unseen Rain: Quatrains of Rumi.* Putney, Vermont: Threshold Books, 1988.

Oseiran, Afif and Alinaqhi Monzavi, editors. *The Letters of Ain-al Qhozat Hamadani.* Tehran, Iran: Asaatir Publications, 1971. Published in 2 volumes. In Farsi.

Pourjavady, N. and P. Lambourn. *The Drunken Universe, an Anthology of Persian Sufi Poetry.* New Lebanon, New York: Omega Publications, 1999.

Sufi. Number 51, Autumn, 2001, pp.10-13.

Saudi Aramco World. November/December 2001. English.

Teresa of Avila, *Interior Castle.* (E. Allison Peers, translator.) From the Critical Edition of P. Silvero de Santa Teresa, C.D. New York: Doubleday, 1989.

Uhlein, Gabriele. *Meditations with Hildegard of Bingen, a Centering Book.* Santa Fe, New Mexico: Bear and Company, Inc., 1983

Further Reading

Barks, Coleman, translator. *The Hand of Poetry, Five Mystic Poets of Persia: Lectures of Inayat Khan*. New Lebanon, New York: Omega Publications, 1993.

Poorjavady, Haleh and Roger Montgomery, Abdol-hossein Pourafzal, Literary Consultant. *The Spiritual Wisdom of Hafez — Teachings of the Philosopher of Love*. Rochester, Vermont: Inner Traditions, 1998.

ABOUT THE AUTHOR

Vraje Abramian, translator, was born in Iran. He is a writer and translator, specializing in the Persian poets of Sufism. He lives in Los Angeles, California. His previous book, *Nobody, Son of Nobody, Poems of Shaikh Abu-Saeed Abil-Kheir* was published by Hohm Press in 2001. He can be contacted c/o Hohm Press, PO Box 2501, Prescott, Arizona, 86302

To receive our catalog, or to order books from Hohm Press, call 800-381-2700.

Visit our website at www.hohmpress.com